CAPE MAY
WALKING TOURS

Short, Fun, No-Stress Tours
for All Ages and Abilities

Michele Paiva

Photography by Jaclyn Paiva-VanWert & Michael VanWert

4880 Lower Valley Road Atglen, Pennsylvania 19310

Schiffer Books are available at special discounts for bulk purchases for sales promotions or premiums. Special editions, including personalized covers, corporate imprints, and excerpts can be created in large quantities for special needs. For more information contact the publisher:

Published by Schiffer Publishing Ltd.
4880 Lower Valley Road
Atglen, PA 19310
Phone: (610) 593-1777; Fax: (610) 593-2002
E-mail: Info@schifferbooks.com

For the largest selection of fine reference books on this and related subjects, please visit our web site at **www.schifferbooks.com**
We are always looking for people to write books on new and related subjects. If you have an idea for a book please contact us at the above address.

This book may be purchased from the publisher.
Include $3.95 for shipping.
Please try your bookstore first.
You may write for a free catalog.

In Europe, Schiffer books are distributed by
Bushwood Books
6 Marksbury Ave.
Kew Gardens
Surrey TW9 4JF England
Phone: 44 (0) 20 8392-8585; Fax: 44 (0) 20 8392-9876
E-mail: info@bushwoodbooks.co.uk
Website: www.bushwoodbooks.co.uk
Free postage in the U.K., Europe; air mail at cost.

Designed by John P.Cheek
Cover design by Bruce Waters
Type set in Seagull Hv BT/Arrus BT

ISBN: 978-0-7643-2946-3
Printed in China

Dedication

I would like to dedicate this book first and foremost to my husband Steve; like a Cape May diamond, our marriage has flowed with the tides, but has become a clear and brilliant treasure with each wave that carries it. I also give honor to my children, Alexandria and Nicholas, for bringing a youthful view on life. I can't help but thank and remember my late parents, for the weekends they brought me to Cape May as a child, and for the tools they gave me to follow dreams.

I, with deep heart, want to dedicate this book to my talented brother, Bob, his stunning and always elegant wife, Kathleen, and his beautiful, successful daughters, Nicole and Jaclyn. I especially honor Jaclyn Paiva-VanWert, and Jaclyn's wonderful husband, Mike VanWert; I'm honored that they are my family and so proud we were able to collaborate on this book together. Cape May is all about family, and this book was born from that very thread, thus I hope this book helps bring your family closer as well.

Acknowledgments

I can't thank the people of Cape May enough. Barb and her delightful staff at the Henry Sawyer Inn gave us a home within the city, nights of the front porch atmosphere, and lazy breakfasts that would tempt us from comforting slumber...Debra at the Chalfonte always had a great story to share and kept me laughing often! There are people in my life who have played an integral role in this book coming to fruition; with a smile, I thank my dear chiropractor, Mitchell Merriam, for without him my hands and shoulders would still look like a Cro-Magnon woman after hours spent typing. Also, kindred spirit, Ms. Lisa Gisone, and her wonderful, spiritual family. To friends, Barb & Hugh Sinn, Karen & Craig Mortzfield, Frank Smith, Dave "Blade" Glarner, Pam Karczeski, Arlene & Heinz Warmhold, my sister-in-law and pal, Terri Lyons; this gang kept me laughing and upbeat through the process, and I appreciate it! I also have to thank my patient and grounding editor and "Diner Diving" partner in crime, Tina. Of course, everyone at Schiffer deserves a huge "thank you" for this opportunity presented – with a special nod to Schiffer editor Jennifer Savage, who is a kindred writing spirit with whom I toiled at a local newspaper, and a nod to my new inspiration, Pete Schiffer, as well. Finally, to Dominic Carnuccio, for keeping my sanity!

Contents

Foreword

Candle lights flicker in darkened windows as a beckoning welcome to visitors today, just as they have for more than 300 years to guide a beloved husband, father, son, or brother back home from the sea.

The Atlantic Ocean and the Delaware Bay define the boundaries of America's oldest seashore resort, Cape May, which sits on Cape Island at the southernmost tip of New Jersey. Long noted for its bountiful fishing, sparkling beaches, pristine surf, and expansive bird sanctuaries, Cape May also embraces the largest collection of Victorian-era homes in America. This distinction is the basis for the city's designation as a National Historic Landmark. These Victorian treasures blend past with present, elegance with amenity, to create beautiful gingerbread homes, hotels, and bed and breakfast inns, providing charm, comfort, welcome, and relaxation to visitors and friends alike.

Cape May, the proud home of the recruit training base for the United States Coast Guard, also boasts a year-round population of 5,000 residents and a myriad of visitors from all corners of the world. For visitors and residents alike, porch sitting and strolling the gas-lit streets of the historic district are Cape May traditions, but all are drawn to the city's shops, tours, theaters, and fine restaurants. The old traditions of the sea remain as fisherman bring the bounty of the sea to market and vacationers fish the bay and deep ocean waters, climb to the top of the Cape May lighthouse, and enjoy the gentle ocean waves. For the land lover, bicycling, birding, golfing, and searching for Cape May diamonds are active pastimes. New traditions and celebrations have been born, making Cape May a year-round resort; the Victorian Christmas, Sherlock Holmes Mystery Weekend, Jazz Festival, Music Festival, Food and Wine Festival are but a few of these. All are imbued with the warmth, history, and enjoyment, which permeate the Cape May experience.

—Barbara Morris
College Professor, Owner, Henry Sawyer Inn,
Cape May, New Jersey

Introduction

After walking Cape May for hours, I noticed one thing. There were no short tours!

There is so much to see in Cape May, that a long tour seems inevitable, so my job, my obligation, was to find a way to showcase Cape May with tours that were short enough not to be cumbersome but unique and detailed enough to provide a sense of history, entertainment, and to exemplify the treasures of Cape May.

This book is broken up into four main tours. All could be completed in one day by the adventure-seeker; however, one or two tours a day is simply a wonderful way to get a taste of the area without taxing your feet!

The photography is unique; you will get a sense that you were right here with us – which is the way we want you to feel – like we are old friends, taking you on a tour of our much-loved home away from home. Even if you don't get to experience all of the tours yourself, or any of the tours even, this book's objective is to bring Cape May to you, either by firsthand experience or through our words and lens.

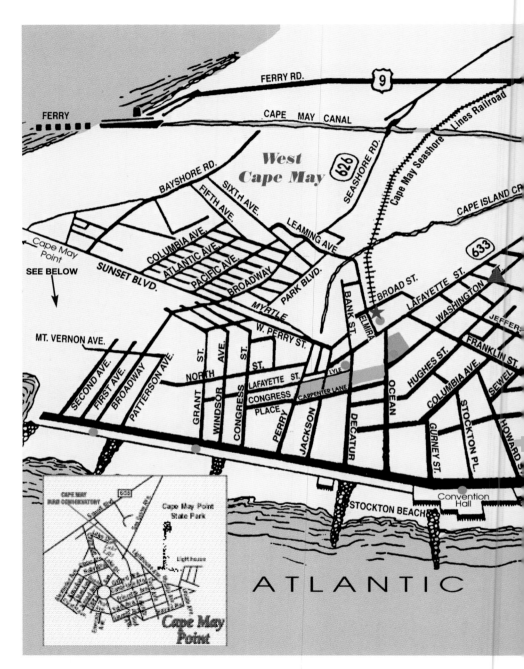

This site is packed with information for anyone visiting Cape May, New Jersey.

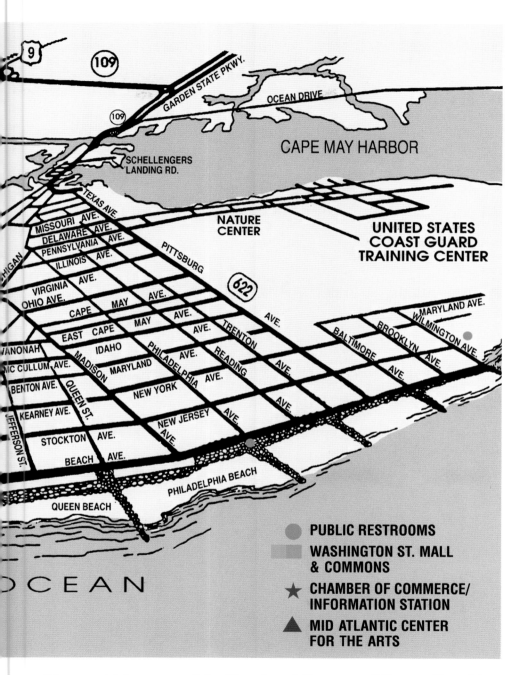

Map provided courtesy of the Chamber of Commerce of Greater Cape May, New Jersey. www.capemaychamber.com

Tour One:
Cape May Point Treasure Hunt

It is always fun to go on a treasure hunt, and all the more so when you are assured of a treasure! Cape May Point is the home of the Cape May Diamonds, treasures to behold. Each night the sea brings the diamond (actually quartz) treasures to the sandy beaches for visitors to scour the sand to find and happily embrace. However, the treasures at the point are plentiful.

We start our tour by traveling from the center of Cape May toward the West, by car, on Sunset Boulevard, which is appropriately named. You will catch glimpses of the most stunning sunsets on this open, unhurried expanse of road.

You'll pass Broadway, Pacific Avenue, Atlantic Avenue, and Columbia Avenue. After passing some adorable homes and more grassland scenery, you will stumble upon a most unique area of Cape May.

Said to be one of the most stunning places to view a sunset, with local lore crediting the sea breezes of the bay for the atmospheric conditions that bring the visual fiesta for the eyes, and a true romantic burst of color that dips into the sea; Sunset Beach at Cape May Point is not to be missed on your trip!

Though you can visit Sunset Beach at anytime, this scenic point is best experienced at dusk. The expansive beach is always filled with rocks and shells for collecting, and you won't have to struggle and squirm for a spot on the shoreline. However, as mentioned, this tour is best experienced a few hours before sundown to get the full effect.

So, drop by in the early evening or stay the day; it is your choice how you want to experience the magic of Cape May Point. Without further delay, let's begin our tour!

Once you park your car in the centrally located lot surrounded by the sea, the shops, and the bay shore, you will start your walking tour by enjoying a game of miniature golf. Where else can you enjoy a relaxing pastime while surrounded by oceanside flora and an ever-crisp breeze to cool you on the hottest days?

Next, you will move on to the very chic Body Boards Shop, complete with beach toys of every color and size, for all ages. Everything from items to make magical sandcastles to activities for shore and sea abound in this charming establishment.

The next stop, just a few lazy steps away, is the shop, Kites, that—though filled with sky-skimming art—is also filled with fossils, rocks, and other biological treasures. It is more of an outdoor mart than a wall-enclosed shop. You'll be mesmerized by the trunks and trunks of shells, which are grouped by style and color. If you want to feel like a kid again, join the other adults and youth who are elbow deep in the trunks trying to find the perfect addition to a collection or who are intent on finding the perfectly shaped sea treasure. Also, you will find garden décor abounds around the perimeter of the shop, so you can bring a bit of the Point to your garden at home.

By now, you are probably hungry. This is a wonderful time to relax at the open air Sunset Beach Grill. The aroma of edible entrées and snacks waft in the air, and the sound of smoothies being mixed bring an eager anticipation of thirst quenching goodness yet to come. You'll be tempted to stop, but don't – not yet! You will come back…. But first…walk…past the shoreline, to the large building across the central lot….

Continue past the shoreline to Sunset Beach Gifts. Though it is a gift shop, you will feel it is more of a museum, with so much to look at! Everything from fine jewelry – and yes, polished Cape May Diamonds set in rings, necklaces, and more – to books, art, décor, and even gourmet coffee line the shelves.

As you stroll back toward the bay, you will notice a large structure that looks like a capsized ship. It looks like a capsized ship because it is just that— a true ship that capsized right there at Cape May Point.

This is the Atlantus, and you will notice it is very close to the shoreline, and that it looks different than most ships you've seen in person or on television. It is unique. The Atlantus was a concrete freighter that is said to have weighed over 3000 tons. Why a concrete ship, you may ask? This ship was one of only twelve, all made of concrete as steel was a hot commodity and very scarce during World War I. The Atlantus, that you see here, was the only one that actually set sail, and it shipwrecked right at the Point, in June of 1926, during a strong storm. What you are looking at is the actual ship, the actual wreck at the actual location. This is a true snapshot of history.

Once you finish with your reverie of the mighty structure of the Atlantus, make your way to the bay shore. You will find one of the most extensive collections of shells, rocks, minerals, and fossils in Cape May, New Jersey, and possibly all of New Jersey, or even the entire eastern seaboard.

If you look hard enough, maybe you will be lucky enough to see the stunning "Cape May Diamonds" we spoke of at the beginning of the tour. The stones, actually in the quartz family, wash ashore and are often polished to such smoothness that they glisten like clear diamonds. Of course, you can take them to a jeweler and have them cut into facets, and they will look all the more diamond-like! The raw form, this natural form of the Cape May Diamond, is actually nature-tumbled, and if you are lucky enough to hold a stone, note that you are holding a biological treasure that was more than a thousand years

in the making through sand contact and movement in the water.

These pure quartz stones come in a variety of sizes, shapes, and even color hues, but most are quite small. Some large stones have been found, some larger than a golf ball! Those larger sizes, it is said, tend to wash ashore more in the winter months; or perhaps, with less people visiting the bay in the winter, there is simply more opportunity to find such a treasure.

If you get your stone polished and faceted, it will have the appearance of a diamond; and many people have done this, finishing the look with the stone mounted in gold or silver.

However, the real pleasure is just looking for a treasures on the beach; the prize is actually the process, as you will meet people from all over the world, all there to find a treasure themselves.

34

Staying in the area, walk toward the flag pole, or catch a seat nearby.

One aspect of this tour is especially heart-warming. Every evening, for over forty years, in the summer season, a flag is lowered to the sound of Taps, and other patriotic music traditions of our country. You may see families, with parents whispering to the children the importance of the flag, or you may see tears rolling down the cheeks of some who have lost loved ones in war.

Across the bay, you will hear the gentle sounds of Americana, as people from all over the United States and abroad, stand in silence, in respect.

The flags that you see have much meaning; they have been donated by families of veterans.

The climax of the evening is the colorful sunset.

It is not unusual to see a real myriad of individuals; families holding hands, couples in embrace, individuals staring across the sea in awe. Almost daily in this dusk hour, you could see a photographer. This is one of the most photographed spots in all of Cape May. Everyone, regardless of whether they come alone, with a family, or with loved one, will be experiencing the same unobstructed, awe-inspiring view of this natural masterpiece. There is silence only to be broken with a few soft "ooooh" and "ahhhs" resounding as the sun lowers and creates vivid colors across the bay. If you experience this, you certainly realize that the real treasure of Cape May Point is the sunset.

TOUR TWO:
Beach Bum Shuffle

There is nothing lazy about the Cape May beaches. You can easily see that they are some of the cleanest, best-kept beaches on the eastern shoreline. Perhaps it is that Southern hospitality at work, and yes, Cape May is in fact, considered a Southern attraction, even though New Jersey is a northeastern state. How did this happen? Well, Cape May is actually below the famous Mason-Dixon Line!

Unlike many beaches in the region, North or South, you can have the ease of the North and the comfort of the South all in one locale. Renting the comforts of home, on the beach, such as chairs, umbrellas, cabanas, and more is easy to do and you'll feel like the beach is a home away from home. Although most of the beaches require tags for a nominal fee, children under twelve do not need tags in most instances.

When on the beach, you can read, relax, explore your artistic sand castle building techniques or swim in the ocean; however, soaking up the sun ranks on most people's list as their number one pastime on the expansive Cape May beaches.

Ever popular is dolphin and whale watching, and you can do this through sea excursions or simply while viewing by the shoreline. Bring your binoculars to experience this event that happens often hour upon hour; but be assured that the dolphins often playfully swim close; you can see them easily with the naked eye. It is actually comical to watch them taunting a dolphin-watching tour boat, while all the people are looking ahead and a school of perhaps seven or fifteen is behind them, following them, giving a real comedic treat to the people on the shore; so be sure, if you take an excursion, to also look behind the boat, not just in front!

Put on your flip-flops, your big sun hat, and let's take the Beach Bum Shuffle!

Find your way to Jefferson Street and make a right onto Beach Avenue.

Your first stop will be the Maycaper Inn, a seaworthy establishment with all the ornamental bells and whistles that any stunning Victorian should have. Be sure to check out the gingerbread quality of the building; this is a common theme in Cape May.

Next, shuffle a few steps further and do not be ashamed if you find yourself staring in awe. The building in front of you, Stockton Manor, decorated with green, cream, and burgundy has been facing the ocean off Cape May for over 130 years. With over 10,000 feet of space, appointed with antiques inside, the building is simply a phenomenal historical landmark.

Designed by architect Stephen D. Button, originally built as a single home for the Baltimore, Maryland, Industrialist Mr. Henry Tatum, this home was one of the largest single homes of it's time in the region.

Button was a prominent Philadelphia architect and he designed many facets of what we consider some of our entire tri-state region's most historic and elaborate buildings, such as several city halls, and several prominent schools and churches in Philadelphia, Pennsylvania, and Camden, New Jersey.

He used a variety of designs, but Button preferred Roman Revival designs. Button died in 1897 in Philadelphia.

Follow your natural inclination to wander to the next mansion, the Hotel Macomber. This mansion resides at the corners of Beach Avenue and Howard Street. This immense building was the largest frame structure of its kind to be built East of the Mississippi River.

This gigantic structure sits upon the former site of the Stockton Hotel, and was rebuilt in 1914. It encompasses four immense stories and the grand shingle style mansion was the last historic landmark built in Cape May.

The Stockton was torn down and the new building that you see here shared space with a church on the same lot. The name has changed only three times. It was first called the Stockton Hotel, then the Stockton Villa when it was rebuilt, and as you see it now, the Hotel Macomber.

Is your stomach growling? In the mood for tuna on a bed of seaweed salad, wonton, and mango wasabi or perhaps you would rather start whetting your appetite with feta and watermelon on a bed of salad dripped with honey vinaigrette? The Union Park Restaurant is where you can enjoy the above delicacies or a beef burger, though of course the burger will be of gourmet quality. Don't forget dessert, especially if you are interested in a sambuca-drenched Venetian! The Union Park Dining Room is under the artistic direction and talent of renowned chef J. Christopher Hubert. Although he changes the menu seasonally, you can be assured during any tour or visit that you will be getting an award winning chef, and upscale and elegant atmosphere intertwined with an inviting family establishment, as he partners with his wife and their family. This is a BYOB establishment. It has been used many times, as its atmosphere lends itself to romance, as a great place to have a wedding as well as a wonderful place to pop "the question!"

Crossing the street, perhaps you want more casual fare; especially if you are a vegetarian. From salads to grilled veggie hoagies, you'll find a variety of choices for your lifestyle. Meat-eaters, don't frown, there is also an array of turkey, burgers, seafood, and roast beef platters at Zoe's. A great break from the beach, or just because, Zoe's is a great place to dress down and enjoy the outdoor eating environment.

What can be more fun for a child, or the child in you, than to create a keepsake from Cape May that is unique. Create-A-Bear is a one-stop shopping craft and keepsake shop where you build your own stuffed animal, completing it's look with accessories, including it's own Cape May swimsuit!

Next door, you will see the 1950s era, "Beach Theatre." This theater is so unique that we have listed it in the "Worth-a-Walk" segment, so be sure to check that section of the book if you are literally standing in front of the building right now! The Beach Theatre is considered a historical monument in Cape May and was one of the most amazing draws of the time, beyond the natural lure of the ocean and shoreline.

Before you turn the corner, you'll find yourself immediately upon, "Down by the Sea," an invigorating little shop with a nautical theme that is a lighthouse lovers delight. With collections of nautical home décor, you will feel at home in this unique shop.

Turn right and proceed onto Gurney Street. Down this street you will find a variety of shops housed within character-filled buildings.

Louie's Pizza is your first stop, right next to the Paint Your Own Pottery studio where any age can create designs to take home and treasure, marking a memorable trip keepsake.

The next stop, a favorite of tourists and locals alike, is the Avalon Café. This is a great place to stop if you would like to get a quick bite to eat and don't have time to waste; that being said, you certainly can sit at the outdoor seating and daydream while watching the life of Cape May wake up in the morning or pass the day by. One thing is for sure, if you do sit at the outdoor café, you will enjoy a never-ending ocean breeze.

After you have enjoyed your micro-roasted batch of coffee and a made-from-scratch pastry at the Avalon Café, it may be time to stop and shop at the beach and fly kites for fun later on your trip, or stop in at Hale Nails to get that perfect manicure to match your swimsuit.

Before we cross the street, check out Shields' Bike Rental. Although walking is fine, biking can be really fun! For a small fee, you can rent by the hour, day or longer. In tourist season, you'll find ditching your car and traveling by foot or by bike is much more enjoyable and efficient.

Shields' has bikes for almost any age and bikes built for one, two or more!

Crossing the street you will notice a row of impeccable Victorians. These are private homes and, though similar, are unique as a grouping. They are in the gingerbread style. This row of homes provides a storybook backdrop that brings a cozy quality to a bustling city shoreline.

As you arrive at the end of Gurney Street where it meets Beach Avenue, you will see a newer building called Avondale by the Sea. This large hotel provides guests with a blend of oceanfront living and city accommodations.

Walking toward the corners of Beach Avenue and Ocean Avenue you will cross the street and walk up the ramp or steps to the ocean-side promenade or sidewalk. There you will experience an even crisper ocean breeze and be privy to a full view of the ocean and endless beach. This area is easily accessible to those in wheelchairs.

At Henry's, you will find a popular eatery for those who tour and those who live in Cape May. This is the only eatery where every seat is the best seat in the house; each seat views the ocean and beaches!

Henry's prides itself on great prices and great food, with a great atmosphere. The open air dining makes you feel like you are right on the beach, yet you are under a fanned roof to keep you cool.

Nearby, the Oasis, a place to grab a gyro, shake, and old-fashioned water ice, is sure to quench your thirst; properly named!

Oh, what a relief! Public bathrooms! ...*And* clean!

Nearby you will see Convention Hall. A recreational hub of activity for Cape May, New Jersey for years, at the time of this writing, they are planning to rebuild the hall, and further develop the entire walk. These are just ideas though that were recently tossed around a city meeting. In either case, Convention Hall will continue to be a central meeting place for tourists and locals to enjoy recreation.

Next door, surrender to the scent of fudge, salt water taffy, nuts, and an assortment of candies at the infamous "Nut House." Straightjacket required if you don't stop in!

Looking for an ooh-la-la outfit? Marie's Clothing, a boutique clothing shop next door to the Nut House, is sure to accessorize your tan in style.

Let your senses awaken to the most delicious fudge, the sought after whipped-cream fudge at the Fudge Kitchen. You'll find an array of special recipe flavors here!

As Al Pacino said in the *Godfather* movie, "Just when I thought I was out they pulled me back in." That is just what you will feel like when you walk by Godfather's, a café that is a welcomed addition to Cape May. Like family, Godfather's Café Italiano is an informal, down to earth eatery that often is referred to as a "Breath of fresh air" by locals, as it offers gourmet choices at affordable prices and options to eat in, or carry out. It is not your usual boardwalk or beach persona in an eatery!

Last but not least, let your hair down and allow your inner-child to run free at Family Fun Arcade. Every age will have a blast here with a myriad of games, including old-fashioned Skee ball!

Remember, the Beach Bum Shuffle covers a relatively small area but, like our other tours, is packed with a combination of unique visuals and a host of activities, food, accommodations, history, culture, and, best of all, the lure of the Cape May beaches, up close and personal. If you visit the beach very early in the morning, like I did, you may walk away with a unique find ... I found, daily, shells that were over seven inches in length. There is always something to see at Cape May, and the Beach Bum Shuffle is a great tour not to miss. It really captures the essence of the beach area of Cape May, New Jersey.

TOUR THREE:
Lover's Lane Stroll

Although families and single individuals will can certainly enjoy this tour, I feel it is best experienced hand-in-hand with someone you love. Think of this as Cape May's lover's lane; truly embrace the passion and romance of a bygone era, even if you only experience this stroll through the pages in this book.

We start our tour at the Henry Sawyer Inn, on Columbia and Franklin. Henry Sawyer was Cape May's Civil War hero. The home is now an Inn, and features a wrap-around porch, with extraordinary historical details still intact, and a character and charm that is unsurpassed. This building has so much history, it is in the Worth-a-Walk section of this book as well. So, if you are looking for more information on the building, be sure to check out that section!

Next stop, the Bacchus Inn, originally the Lewis Tannenbaum home. This home is a Gothic Revival style, which was built by local developer, Peter McCollum. Currently, the Inn has a theme of romance and wine, which is unique to the area. Guest rooms named after distinct wine regions and varieties, such as Tuscany and Zinfandel, are par for the course in this cultured inn.

Take a few steps down to Howard Street to the Chalfonte. This cultural icon in Cape May is also featured in the Worth-a-Walk section of this book as it has a most unique background.

This impressive building contains many decorative elements, including a large veranda; as you stand in front of this impressive building, note that you are in the presence of Cape May's oldest hotel.

Bringing yourself back to Columbia, you will notice at the address 715 what is now known as the Ashley Victorian Inn, formally the John Tack residence. This home is Gothic in style, with intricate bric-a-brac and a perfect wrap-around porch.

Not much is known about John Tack, except that he was born in September of 1799 and died in July 1885 in Cape May. It is believed that he married a young lady by the name of Sarah Dunn.

Walking the corner and making a right, continue to Hughes Street. Without crossing Hughes Street, walk to the corner of Hughes and Franklin so that you are looking at 665 Hughes Street. This is a unique private home and, aside from the architecture, you'll enjoy the decorative but well-used hitching post still standing and in excellent condition.

All the way down from 659 through 651, the private residences are noteworthy. Notice small rooms if you can peek from the road (don't trespass!) that are not flush with the home exterior walls. Flush is certainly the befitting word all right; these rooms were originally the first indoor plumbing styles, if you can call it that, on the second floors. Essentially, they are outhouses on stilts! Yet, even more enthralling are the exuberant colors that you will view here. Notice the marriage of yellows and oranges, and nuances of blues, greens, and purples.

At 644, you'll notice a building with a plain sign, the "Girls-Friend-ly-Society." Behold the last wooden hotel! Owned by the Episcopal Church, it is still used as a female-only summer residence and is called the Holiday House.

The Joseph Hall Cottage is a vision of art with wrought iron, elaborate architecture, and character. This private home is simply stunning.

Next door, another sight is "The Cherry House." Built in 1849, this home boasts a Federal style and something more unique, the original front door.

Continue down Hughes Street if you please, or you could end your tour with dinner at the Chalfonte.

If you continue to stroll down Hughes Street, you will be privy to one of the most original, well-kept, loved, and historic streets in our country. The elegant street boasts bungalows, a variety of Victorians, a myriad of architecture, elaborate gardens, quiet serenity, and, of course, always a place to fall in love, over and over again.

Tour Four:
Shop 'til You Drop

Amidst the storybook homes and soaring Victorian mansions, toward the expansive beaches and mingling between historical streets, arises a concentrated shopping bonanza.

Like all of our tours, the Shop 'til You Drop tour is easy on the feet, stays in the same area of interest, and is a feast for the senses. You'll be enticed by the aroma of slow-cooking meals that are reminiscent of a Parisian cobblestone bistro, and see the same high-level of art that you'd find in a Rome art district, coupled with the shopping of Milan. A true melting pot for the senses will awaken you on this encompassing tour.

We will start on the corner of Carpenter and Ocean Streets, where you will find yourself immersed in a bevy of bakeries dotted between the shops within eyesight.

You will see Kohr Bros., a famous beach ice cream shop with historical ties. It all started in 1917, when a young man from York, Pennsylvania, purchased an ice cream machine. The young man, Archie Kohr, along with his brothers, Elton and Lester, lived on a dairy farm and simply wanted to expand their business. This was a hit; not only did they make the ice cream but delivered it door-to-door along with the milk deliveries.

In trying to develop a lighter, less fatty ice cream, the Kohr family stumbled upon something—a unique, silky treat that was unlike anything they had ever experienced. They set up a booth in 1919 on Coney Island, and sold more than 18,000 cones at a nickel each; a business was born!

In 1927, Kohr Bros. starting setting up stores throughout the East Coast, in ten states. Cape May, New Jersey, is home to one of the stores where you can experience the silky, cold ice cream yourself!

Across the street, temptation hits harder with the aroma of sweetness sifting through the ocean breeze from the popular Fudge Kitchen.

Going to the next block, you must stop into one of Cape May's urban hot spots, The Ugly Mug. Here you will find a true mix of tourists and locals, and it is considered the Cape May melting pot!

From burgers topped with crabmeat to crayons and paper for kids, this is a great casual experience that makes a fan out of nearly every visitor!

Nature calling? Here you will find relief at the public restrooms!

Not just a container of heaven, but a shop you can visit; cool off with one of the unique recipes at Ben & Jerry's, a unique franchise started by two men who have a hippie-quality and a company that was eco and green long before it was trendy.

Across the walk, you will find everything from inexpensive trinkets and an array of clothing to elite jewels and art at City Centre Hall.

Coming out of the mall, continue to the corner of Jackson Street.

This block is simply packed with a myriad of shops. What you'll love here is that art focus sprinkled between amazing places to quench your desires and thirst!

Wave One, a great shop not to miss…

...not to be confused with Making Waves.

After shopping, you may want to cross Perry Street and check out the Victorian Motel, known as the "best location in Cape May" by many tourists for the fact that it is nestled between shops, eateries, the ocean, and a short walk to the historic districts.

After shopping, don't drop just yet, you can continue and explore the many shops spawning this shopping epicenter or drop in at the Victorian Motel to spend a night recouping from all of that shopping!

Although this is a short walk "on paper," you will notice that actually walking it could take longer than any of the tours just for the logistics. You will be stopping for longer sessions, exploring the nuances of the stores, eateries, and galleries. Reminding yourself to venture out of the mall area is going to be easy, as with every few steps you take in Cape May there are plenty of things to see, places to shop, places to eat, and views to take in.

Because there are a few notable attractions, we decided to give you a walking tour of places that would be "Worth-a-Walk" unto themselves, with more detailed information on each. Our next chapter is devoted to this handful of establishments. Enjoy!

Worth-a-Walk Attractions

As we have mentioned, there are so many unique attractions of historical and cultural value within Cape May, New Jersey, that it would be impossible to include them all. However, we found a few locations, some which are within our tours, some not, that are worth a walk unto themselves. Please try to visit them while in Cape May, New Jersey!

Congress Hall

Our first attraction is Congress Hall. Located on 251 Beach Avenue, Congress Hall is not just a spa-like hotel. It is a spectacular, sprawling icon of history for the area.

It's start in the early part of 1800 was that of a simplistic boarding house, for the most part, to accommodate visitors to Cape May. The owner at the time, Thomas Hughes, is said to have called his boarding home the "big house." It is rumored that the locals thought Hughes to be silly and perhaps a little egotistical, and nicknamed the hotel, "Tommy's Folly."

What made this hotel unique is the large shared dining room for all of the guests and simplistic walls, woodwork, and accommodations.

The name changed from The Big House to Congress Hall when Hughes was elected to Congress; this commenced in 1828.

Though large, the growth continued; the building doubled in size in years to follow, to accommodate the popularity of both Cape May and Congress Hall as a destination and accommodation.

A fire that destroyed the building in 1878 did not end its life; it was rebuilt and was a popular retreat for politicians and other noteworthy men and women. Congress Hall was a summer retreat for composer John Phillip Sousa, along with Ulysses S. Grant, Franklin Pierce, and James Buchanan. Even President Benjamin Harrison is noted to have called the structure his "Summer White House."

One exciting boast that Congress Hall can declare is having the first post-Prohibition cocktail bar in Cape May, which opened in 1934. If you happen to venture into what is now known as the Brown Room, you will be standing in the space that was in fact that cocktail bar.

Although many of Cape May's landmarks have been saved to the best of their ability, the new owners, who purchased the building in 1995, have been giving the Hall a complete renovation and, according to their site (***Their website? Or material provided at the reconstruction site itself? Thanks.**), with the goal of returning Congress Hall to it's "former glory." As you can see, the site is stunning, and now, instead of bare walls and roughing it to be at the beach, most visitors will attest to its highly spa-like atmosphere, complete with dining, gift shops, yoga, business facilities, and a children's program, to name a few.

Cape May Lighthouse

If you are going to visit Cape May, New Jersey, you won't want to miss the Cape May Lighthouse. It sits within Cape May Pointe State Park, and is the third documented lighthouse at the southern tip of New Jersey, constructed in 1859. However, the original lighthouse was built in 1823, with the second in 1847.

Standing almost 158 feet tall, this lighthouse is stunning.

It is now automated; the last keeper of the lighthouse retired in 1930. In the twentieth century, it is said that the average keeper made about $600 a year.

The Mid-Atlantic Center for the Arts, known as MAC, won a lease to restore and renovate the lighthouse from the Coast Guard in 1986. More than a decade later, and approximately $2 million dollars in grants, the restoration is not totally complete; there are always renovations and upgrades to tend to. In 1992, the lighthouse was transferred from the Coast Guard to the State of New Jersey.

There were even archaeological studies and investigations through some of the property, including the walkways. What you see now, in front of you, is the original color scheme. The lighthouse is as close to authentic as it can get while remaining within safety ranges for visitors.

If you have the endurance, you can climb the 218 steps – with almost 200 of them being in the iron spiral staircase within the tower – to reach the top of the lighthouse; however, many visitors enjoy the lighthouse from the ground. There is plenty to learn at the visitor site, without the climb!

You may be interested to know that the keeper and his family used to live at the lighthouse site. In 1902, the family site area was enlarged to provide more space for the families.

Fisherman's Memorial

This statue is a bittersweet reminder of the seamen who went to sea, and the women and children who waited for their return; some waited a lifetime. This can't be missed at the nook and fishing wharf area.

Beach Theatre

The Beach Theatre has an awesome history and, in the words of Barbara Skinner – an expert on the Beach Theatre since the day it opened on June 29th, 1950 – it has been an integral part of Cape May's artistic community.

The theatre was designed by famous architect William H. Lee. Born in Shamokin, Pennsylvania, Lee was a famous theatre and academic building architect. He designed some of the buildings of Temple University, and worked for Franklin and Marshall College as

well as serving as the chief architect for Eastern Baptist Theological Seminary. He was a very community-involved individual; one of his notable outreach endeavors was serving as a founding member of the Philadelphia Police Athletic League.

According to Skinner, Lee had designed over forty theaters, with the Beach Theatre being one of the last projects in his career.

The Beach Theatre was under attack in the not-so-distant past, facing the possible threat of demolition. However, the Beach Theatre

Foundation was founded, with the following mission: "The Beach Theatre Foundation, Inc. is a not-for-profit organization formed to preserve and restore the historically authenticated Beach Theatre in Cape May, New Jersey, and utilize the complex as a state-of-the-art showcase for cinema and the arts.

Excellence in a diverse array of films will be the hallmark of the theatre for the cultural benefit of the residents of Cape May, Southern New Jersey, and visitors from around the world. The foundation's visionary goal is to establish the Beach Theatre and Cape May as an internationally recognized center for film history, film preservation & restoration, independent filmmaking, and film education."

If you would like to help preserve this local attraction, historic site, and national treasure, visit www.beachtheatre.org for more information, news, captivating photos, and biographies of founders, designers, and notable movie screenings.

Henry Sawyer Inn

This book would not be complete without a look at the beginning of Cape May, through the beauty of the humble, but historical, Henry Sawyer Inn.

Barbara and Mary Morris, Innkeepers, outline that The Henry Sawyer Inn was built in 1877 by Eldridge Johnson, then the treasurer of Cape May, president of the Cape May Savings and Building Association, and trustee of the Presbyterian Church.

Mr. Johnson purchased the property on which he built his home from Henry Sawyer, Cape May's Civil War hero, builder, and proprietor of the Chalfonte Hotel, and Cape May city councilman.

Eldridge Johnson lived in this home for thirty-three years during his long and unique career of public leadership in Cape May.

A plaque on the inn, directly to the left of the front door, commemorates Mr. Johnson. The inn is named for Mr. Sawyer and rooms at the inn are named for the ladies in the Johnson & Sawyer families. This home, single-handedly, has one of the most unique and prosperous foundations in all of Cape May, simply by the association of two of the most powerful men in Cape May history.

The building is now a bed and breakfast, with an extensive antique and collectible collection, common rooms, and a wrap around front porch. Be sure to view the original windows, which are rare in a beach home of this stature.

In Closing

In closing, I wish to give honor to the many websites, books, and people who were a part of this project, for without them, this project would not be.

ADC, The Map People. *Cape May County New Jersey Map.* Duncan, South Carolina: Langenscheidt Publishing Group, n.d.

Chamber of Commerce. *Cape May NJ, A Visitors Guide.* Cape May, New Jersey: Chamber of Commerce, n.d.

Exit Zero Publishing. *Cool Cape May.* Rio Grande, New Jersey: Exit Zero Publishing, 2007.

Jordan, Joe J. *Three Walking Tours of Historic Cottages, Cape May Point.* Atglen, Pennsylvania: Schiffer Publishing, 2004.

Macken, Lynda Lee. *Haunted Cape May.* New Jersey: Black Cat Press, 2002.

McCarthy, Mary & Bruce M. Minnix. *Cape May for All Seasons.* Preservation Media, 1998.

Salvini, Emil. *The Summer City by the Sea: Cape May, New Jersey, An Illustrated History.* New Brunswick, New Jersey: Rutgers University Press, 1995.

Skinner, Tina & Bruce Waters. *Cape May's Gingerbread Gems.* Atglen, Pennsylvania: Schiffer Publishing, 2004.

www.beachtheatre.org
www.capemaychamber.com
www.capemaycity.com
www.capemaycountyherald.com
www.capemaymac.org
www.capemaywhalewatcher.com
www.capenet.com
www.thebeachcomber.com
www.thejerseycape.com
Cape May Pointe
The Beach Theatre
The Chalfonte
The Henry Sawyer Inn & Library at the Henry Sawyer Inn